Fear!
No More!

by Pastor Lee Martinez

Fear! No More!
By Pastor Lee Martinez

ISBN # 978-0-9986992-9-5

Edited by Eli Gonzalez
Book Design by Ymmy Marketing

For information address inquiries to:
tcwfpastorlee@gmail.com
or
www.theghostpublishing.com

Printed in USA

Dedication

I want to dedicate this work to my Pastor, best friend, armor bearer, watchtower, wife, and life partner. Michelle, thank you for always believing in me, even when I couldn't believe in myself.

I love you baby.

Foreword
by Pastor Jay Patrick

Fear No More is a must read for anyone that is hanging in the balances of God's promise of victory and the enemy's plans of defeat. Pastor Lee Martinez has penned a book that will help you win the battle in your mind of fear and insecurity.

Second Corinthians 2:11 is very clear that the only way Satan can get an advantage over us is if we are ignorant of his devices. Satan's chief device and tool of mass destruction is often very subtle and can go undetected for an entire lifetime, it's called FEAR.

Dr. Myles Monroe once said the wealthiest place on the planet is a cemetery because it is full of untapped potential, ideas never executed, inventions never researched, businesses never started, books that were never written, and so much more. Pastor Lee has initiated this very important dialogue to end this vicious cycle.

It is my prayer that as you flip through these pages, you will get revelation and strategy on how to face and defeat your deepest fears. You deserve to live your best life, free from the crippling bondage of fear. A life that experiences the freedom and liberty that Jesus Christ intended us all to have.

I have experienced Pastor Lee's ministry in Boston, MA and saw firsthand how uniquely graced he and his wife are for deliverance and breaking of cycles of dysfunction. Their mantle is deliverance from darkness, namely fear. There is such a freedom in their ministry, and I know this literary work is just an extension of what their ministry DNA consists of.

I have worked with pastors all over the country, and I am confident that there are few more prepared and focused on tackling this subject and exposing a dimension of darkness and warfare that is often overlooked and disguised with great denial.

Get Ready To FEAR NO MORE!!!!

Pastor Jay Patrick

Author of, The Millennial Manual and, Church Leadership Moments: 21 Things Every Pastor Wants To Say To Their Congregation

Introduction

There's a saying that if you do what you love, you will never work a day in your life. What I have experienced is that if you do what you have been called by God to do, you will never live an empty day in your life.

God has called me to preach His marvelous gospel since I was 13 years old. It is my passion to work for God and to be His instrument in setting captives free. Since the days of my youth, He has used me in the realm of spiritual warfare and the ministry of deliverance. I have been ministering for nearly 25 years all over the Northeast and in Puerto Rico. One thing has been proven time and time again - there is still power, salvation, healing, deliverance, and freedom in the name of Jesus!

To me, nothing compares to witnessing to someone who had been bound for a long time and who was at the end of their rope, as if they were even afraid to have hope, and see the love of Christ pull them out of that darkness. I live for those precious moments. Along with my wife and kids, it is the very essence that helps me get up every morning with a hop in my step and a smile on my face.

You have to understand, I was once one of those people. I had felt bound, condemned by my mistakes, and abandoned by those who said they would be there for me. But when I thought I was outside of the realm of redemption, when I thought I would live a life of spiritual defeat, when I had experienced pain so deep that I felt all the love I once had was gone - the love of God reached me. He shifted my mindset. He delivered me from a destructive destiny. He gave me purpose. I learned that if God did it for me, He could do it for anyone else, He can do it for you!

I have been called to transfer a revelation God gave me into written form with a specific goal in mind: *I want you to experience a deeper level of deliverance.*

Many times we believe we know what is wrong with us and what we need to be freed from. Without realizing that the things we've identified as our problems come from deeper rooted issues. Unknowingly, we battle against strongholds and a strongman. But I'm here to call out the spirit of fear as the source of our actual problems, and I want to share with you how to detect it and how to defeat it.

I've had the privilege to minister in countless churches and to countless souls, and everywhere I've gone, I've encountered people who are tired of living in the spiritual, emotional, and even the physical condition they find themselves in. They hear about a God of love, power, and deliverance being preached, but still find themselves in a state of bondage. The problem is, although they believe God is mighty, they don't believe that He can do powerful things in their lives.

That's probably the reason why you grabbed this book and have invested money and time to read it. You saw the cover. You read the title and recognized your condition in it. My hope is that when you are done reading this book, you will get the revelation of the source of your bondage and your mindset shifts to understanding you are not sentenced to staying in that condition. I believe, with all my being, that you will also receive the revelation of how to be delivered from your bondage.

You have just embarked on a journey, whether you realize it or not. Along the way, areas may be touched that you had buried deep down within you. Festering wounds that you had decided never to deal with again. In this journey, you may have to face things that have happened to you in the past that could bring out emotions you never wanted to encounter again. Before you begin, I'm going to encourage you to stay strong and be open and honest with yourself. I truly believe that by the end of this journey, you will find deliverance

10 *Pastor Lee Martinez*

through the blood of Christ, and through His Word. The Holy Spirit will be with you, from the beginning of this journey, to console you, heal you, and guide you to the other side called FREEDOM.

It's time that you look at the spirit of fear right square in the eyes and say, "Fear. No More!

Pastor Lee Martinez

Table of Contents

Chapter 1

What is Fear?

A toddler has just learned how to take its first steps. The little lad begins to walk, back and forth, from one parent's arms to the other. The child is excited because he can now move from one place to another on his own volition, and the parents are proud to see their child advancing in his growth. But one afternoon, when the parents are not looking, the child attempts, with confidence, to walk on his own. After taking a couple of steps, he trips and falls. He begins to cry with all his might; the way children cry when they feel real pain.

The next several days, the child's parents find it hard to understand why their son doesn't attempt to walk on his own again. The little boy is now afraid to walk because of the traumatic event he experienced. He never realized it, neither did his parents, that he has just experienced his first encounter with **FEAR.**

Fear is a part of life. We have all experienced some form of fear; fear of heights, fear of riding a roller coaster, fear of the dark, etc. However, fear is not only normal, it's also necessary. It's designed to help us distinguish between things that are dangerous from what is safe as we grow older. It's going through experiences like this that we now know not to put our hands on top of a hot stove.

Our bodies have an instinctive reaction to fear and volatile situations called the "fight or flight" response, where certain chemicals in our bodies and certain body parts react in a way that allows us to either escape or face the danger head on. But there is a difference between this fear and the fear that the Apostle Paul wrote to Timothy about.

The enemy roars in order to intimidate us

Fear is one of the devil's most prolific and powerful weapons. It's why I believe that the Holy Spirit inspired Peter to write: 'the devil is walking as a roaring lion, looking for whom to devour.' The enemy roars in order to intimidate us, to see if we allow his threats to open the door to fear in our lives. Satan uses fear to paralyze us.

The enemy will use fear to tell us we have no business thinking and believing we can be blessed and favored to be good husbands, wives, business owners, graduates, and even saved. No matter how many times a preacher or pastor delivers a sermon on the fact that salvation is FREE and accessible to all who believe, fear will tell you that salvation is not for you because you have the inability to be faithful enough or persistent enough to win the race to eternal life. Our adversary has used fear to keep us from submitting to our wives and husbands by reminding us of our past experiences and telling us that if we give one hundred percent to our spouses, they will hurt us, mishandle us, and break our hearts the way others have done.

Being A Spectator

Have you noticed how many times we say we're scared of something without actually trying it first? How can it be that we would be so afraid of something without even having experienced it? How are you scared of marriage if you've never been married? How are you afraid of failing in your business when you never started a business? Why do you walk around with such fear and anxiety that you will fail God when He already paid the price for you?

The answers lie within the experiences you have been through. At first glance, they seem to have nothing to do with one another. But the enemy strategically uses past encounters and traumatic experiences that marked you in such a way that they become a home base to the spirit of fear that is trying to dominate and overtake your life.

This becomes critical to your faith-walk, because now your perspective, the way you view your life is based on encounters and experiences, which you were witnesses to but were not necessarily a partaker in, or the main character. We become like the guy who's scared to get on a roller coaster ride. When the person is asked if they ever been on, they say "no."

How did I get up here?

In the spring of 2017, I took a vacation to Florida with 3 of my sons, my best friend and Associate Pastor, Juan (we call him Bam Bam), his two sons, and Alex, my good friend and head of security. We decided to go to an amusement park in Kissimmee. As we were walking around, we saw a ride called Sky Coaster. It had a rope, with 3 people strapped to it. They were lying down, superman style, before being released from an altitude of 500 feet. When we all looked up at it, we said, "heck no. I'm not getting on that thing." It fascinated us so we watched as people would get on and fly over our heads screaming from the top of their lungs. The more we watched, the less inclined we were to get on.

As the day wore on, we began to challenge each other to get on the ride. Do you know what happens when men challenge each other to a dare? You end up strapped to a jacket, held up by two ropes, next to your firstborn son, and your over 220 pounds, 6 foot tall, head of security. The ironic and quite funny part is that the head of security seemed to be the one that was most afraid. As the rope began to pull us higher and higher, the people and the rest of the rides became smaller and smaller. As I got close to the 500-foot altitude, I began asking myself "what am I doing here? How did I get up here?"

Before we got on, the ride operator informed us that someone had to be in charge of pulling the cord that would release us from that height, to get us to soar across the sky. We had decided it would be me.

I clearly did not want to be there. But as we were locked in place, I realized that if I wanted to get down, I had the power in my hands. So, I composed myself and took hold of the situation. I didn't vanquish the fear. It was very real. However, in spite of the fear, I pulled the cord. And there we went, soaring across the sky like birds!

Was it scary? Yes. But it was also a fantastic experience. When we got off, Alex, who initially was more afraid than anyone said: "I would do it again."

I use this story to bring you a spiritual revelation. Many times, the enemy will make us afraid of something (marriage, being a business owner, being a strong Christian) before we even get a chance to try it or walk into it. The enemy knows that if we were to overcome our fears and go forward, through the anointing of the Holy Ghost, we would conquer every generational curse and grab every promise and blessing that the Lord has spoken over our lives!

Strongholds

"For the weapons of our warfare are not carnal, but mighty through God to the bringing down of strongholds."

2 Corinthians 10:4.

The word for stronghold, in the Greek, is *ochumara,* which means to fortify, through the idea of holding safely; a castle.

The apostle Paul was a very meticulous writer. If Paul were talking about demons, he would've stated, "to the bringing down of demons." When Paul is talking about strongholds, he is not speaking about demons. He is speaking about a fortified place that is used to protect and store life-sustaining materials.

Strongholds are traumatic situations that we have been through that scared us so much we've created walls to 'protect us,' brick by brick. Events like divorces, broken relationships, physical abuse, emotional abuse, or mental abuse. Many of these events have happened in our lives, yet we have not brought them to the cross, or believe them to be in our past.

Traumatic events have aligned themselves as bricks laid one on top of the other, and have created strongholds or fortresses of fear within us. The strongholds become storehouses for spirits like fear, generational curses, and other demonic presences. Strongholds become the habitation for the spirit of depression, the spirit of anger, the spirit of lust, and even to addictions such as pornography, alcohol, and drugs.

The purpose of strongholds is for the enemy to create a place where nothing or no one can come in unless it belongs to that camp. Like a castle door is brought down by two big chains in order to let something in or out, is the same principles the enemy uses strongholds. He tries to control the traffic that comes in and out of your spirit, soul, and in some instances, even your body.

Strongholds become the place where the spirit of fear not only hides but also lives and thrives. The strongholds, these events, are now being used in our lives as protected walls to stay bound to the spirit of fear. That is why when someone is asked why he or she is afraid, a common answer is, "because of what I've been through." A broken relationship, if not given to the Lord to help us heal and forgive, will turn into the place or stronghold in which we store a spirit of un-forgiveness, bitterness, or loneliness.

Let me make myself clear: the devil does not have the power nor the authority to impose his will on us. Only God has that type of power and authority. But because His desire is for us to serve Him willingly, He does not impose His will on us.

The devil does not have the power nor the authority to impose his will on us

---

Many times these events are life choices or circumstances that we go through. Some are self-inflicted, but others are the results of other people's decisions or lack thereof. As children, we had no control over the brokenness, abuse, and dysfunction that was present in our parent's marriage. But their decisions and behaviors influenced and created events and situations in our lives as children that the enemy has used to develop strongholds that are still present to this day in our lives.

When I have ministered to other people change, forgiveness, and advancement, with frustration in their voices, they implore for me to understand them, "Pastor, but you don't know what I've been through." The truth is, it is not me that doesn't understand, it's them. What has happened to them has formed their reasoning to stay in the condition that they're in, be it spiritual, emotional, or even physical turmoil.

The devil has transformed these events that you have been a participant in or spectator to and has transformed them into strongholds that now have made you feel that you must live captive to your condition. This is also why it becomes difficult for some suffering from demonic oppression or possession to be freed of them. Many times we believe that this is just the way they are, that this is a part of their character. We haven't arrived at the realization that spirits have formed strongholds within them. It's why, in occasions, it becomes difficult to rebuke demons from those people.

Sometimes we are not aware that it isn't part of our character and it's not just the way we are. Events we've been through have created strongholds that store spirits of anger, bitterness, and loneliness. Our inward condition projects outwardly in the way we speak and in how we interact with others.

Paul asks, "how can we get rid of a spirit when it's hiding behind a stronghold?" He answers the question by telling us our weapons of our warfare are not carnal but are strong and mighty for the breaking down of strongholds!

The weapons of our warfare are mighty because they have the power and the ability to bring down those events we've been through that marked us in such a way that has us behaving in ways we don't want to.

God is reminding you today, "I gave you the power. I gave you weapons so mighty that you will no longer have to try to rebuke the spirits of anger or bitterness out of your life. When you activate those weapons of warfare, you will bring down the strongholds and those spirits will no longer have a place where to live or hide.

And when this happens, they will have to flee in the name of Jesus Christ, our Lord! They will no longer have a place of residence within you. You don't have to track down Televangelists or an Internet Prophet to lay hands on you for you to be free of a vile spirit. You don't have to find the nearest Camp Meeting or Revival Service to receive your deliverance. All you need is the weapons of warfare God gave you to bring down the strongholds.

What about the promises you made me?

One morning as I was in prayer I began to ask God, "where are all the promises that you promised me? Why aren't they coming to pass? I know your word says you are not a Son of Man to lie nor the Son of Man to repent. But I don't see coming to pass what has been spoken over my life."

That morning, the spirit of the Lord spoke to me, "why are you asking me about these things?"

I thought, *Huh? What do you mean why am I asking you? You're my Lord, aren't you the one I'm supposed to be asking?*

The spirit of the Lord told me, "I don't have what you're asking me for."

I was starting to believe I needed to stop praying and get something to eat because I thought my hunger must have been affecting my mind. But then the spirit of the Lord told me this: "My son, I already gave it to you. The issue is you allowed the devil to take it from you."

This train of thought was in me because of strongholds that were still present in my life

---

Without realizing it, I had allowed the enemy to come and rob me of the promises that God had given me. He then stored them inside the strongholds I allowed him to create within me. So when it was time for me to walk into a promise that God had given me, I would allow thoughts of insufficiency, inadequacy, and doubt to paralyze me. I began to realize that this train of thought was in me because of strongholds that were still present in my life. You see, many of the things that God promised you he has already released them into the atmosphere and into your life.

But the strongholds that are present in your life don't allow you to feel as if you can walk into them and operate in them. So not only are curses and spirits stored in the strongholds, but the enemy also uses the strongholds to store the promises and blessings that he has stolen from you. That's why Jesus said, "The kingdom of God is within you." The Holy Spirit is ministering to you today telling you to stop looking up and start looking within.

Chapter 2

The Strong Man

Why does the enemy use the Strongholds Strategy? Because he's a copycat. He knows Christ Jesus is establishing the kingdom of God within you. His job is to construct, brick by brick and layer by layer, an opposing kingdom. Christ establishes his kingdom by getting us to understand that our past was crucified on the cross with him. That God's kingdom shall be established within us in the present through the revelation of who we are and who we will be in the future.

The enemy's counter move is to establish the opposing kingdom based on the past, and to get you to a place to live based on this kingdom, in your present.

Galatians 5:17 says it like this: "for the desires of the flesh are against the Spirit, and the desires of the Spirit are against the flesh, for these are opposed to each other, to keep you from doing the thing you want to do." You see, your Spirit is an agent of the kingdom of heaven. Your flesh is an agent of the kingdom of darkness.

The enemy uses the flesh to force you to see things in the temporal. Paul writes in 2nd Corinthians 10:4, for the weapons of our warfare are not carnal. The word carnal, in the Greek language, is *'sarkikos,' which means temporal*. The word temporal means something related to worldly as opposed to spiritual affairs, secular. The flesh's assignment is to get us to filter everything we believe in through a temporal (worldly or secular) view.

Strongholds are implanted in our lives when we allow our flesh to have its way. Here is where our hurts, pains, generational curses, and addictions, are stored. It's also where our hopes, dreams, and aspirations the enemy has stolen from us are, putting our futures at risk.

In Matthew 12:29 and 30, Jesus, speaking to the scribes that were accusing him of casting out devils in the name of Beelzebub, said, "how can someone enter a strong man's house and plunder his goods, unless he first binds the strong man? Then indeed he may plunder his house."

Although Jesus only seems to be addressing the fact that it is impossible for him to be casting out the devil in the name of the devil, I believe that he is also giving us a glimpse into the spirit realm. The enemy uses strongholds to store up everything that we have mentioned. But I believe that the enemy also places a strong man to live and protect the entrance to the strongholds. This Strong Man is called the spirit of fear.

The strong man of fear uses the characteristic of intimidation to scare us away from even trying to retake what was stolen from us. It is no coincidence that in his teachings, Jesus uses the term *kingdom of God* and *kingdom of heaven*. Every kingdom has a castle, guards, soldiers, and a form of currency. It has people who submit to the rulers of the kingdom, generals who lead the army, and a king.

You are a castle in the kingdom of God. The angels are the guards according to Psalms 91:11. Your words are the currency according to Proverbs 18:21. The citizens of the kingdom make up Jesus' bride. The archangels are the generals that lead the army according to Revelation 12:7-9. And Christ Jesus, the King of Kings and Lord of Lords rules as the king according to Revelation 19:1-16.

What is in your hand?

We must now hear the word of the Lord, the way Moses did when God said to him, "what is in your hand?" (Exodus 4:2) Moses replied, "a staff." Much later in Moses' life, as written in Exodus 14:15, we see God ask Moses, "Why do you cry to me? Lift up your staff, and stretch out your hand over the sea and divide it, that the people of Israel may go through the sea on dry ground."

Let's get a little deeper and see with our spiritual eyes what had actually transpired. When Moses was speaking to God through the burning bush, he shared with God his fear that the people would not believe him. God asked him, "What is in your hand?"

---

*The staff represented a shift
in his destiny*

When Moses looked at what he was holding, he sees a staff. To Moses, the staff represented a shift in his destiny, a shift in his future. By all accounts, Moses, who was raised as a Prince of Egypt, had a blessed upbringing in the sense that he didn't want for anything. However, because of decisions he had made, he was forced to leave that kingdom.

The staff was the representation of how being exiled of one kingdom gave way to the entrance of another. The staff represented how everything that he had been through had set him up to have power and authority that was higher and mightier than the kingdom that he used to belong to.

God is asking you, what's in your hand? Do you know? Do you see the power and authority God has given you? Do you realize the calling He has for you? God's destiny for you is why the enemy is so hell-bent on turning the circumstances, events, and traumatic situations that you have been through into prisons of despair deep within you. He knows, that if God were to get a hold of those memories, those doubts, those feelings of inadequacies, and those feelings of resentment, He would change the course of your life. He would take that which the enemy designed to hurt you and turn them into a staff, a weapon of warfare that you will be able to use to bring down strongholds, not only in your life but also in other people's lives who find themselves bound! Glory to God!

Again, God is asking you, what is in your hands?

The Truth about The Cross

The Bible declares in Matthew 16:24-26, "then Jesus told the disciples, 'if anyone would come after me, let him deny himself and take up his cross and follow me. For whoever would save his life will lose it, but whoever loses his life for my sake will find it."

Notice in this verse God is speaking about picking up the cross, denying himself, and losing his life. Paul says in 2nd Timothy 2:4, "no one serving as a soldier gets entangled in civilian affairs, for then they cannot please the officer who enlisted them." We've always spoken about picking up the cross, thinking that it was only meant to put it up on our shoulders. But for years, decades, and maybe even a century or two, the church might have had an incorrect perspective on the cross.

Many in the church view the cross as a chore, as something that slows us down, as a burden. But, if you turn your cross upside down and hold it, it can be wielded like a huge, mighty, and terrible sword! Come on somebody!

The enemy knows that if you submerge yourself in the presence of God your divorce will become a weapon. He knows that your miscarriage will become a weapon. Your pass addictions will become a weapon. The times you've lied will become a weapon. The times you've gotten drunk will become a weapon. The times you've cheated will become a weapon. The times you've physically hurt someone will become a weapon. The foul words that have come out of your mouth will become a weapon. The bad examples you've given your children will become a weapon.

It's time to change what you thought you know of the cross and understand that you carry a weapon

---

It's time to change what you thought you know of the cross and understand that you carry a weapon. With the sword of your cross in one hand and the double-edged sword of the Word of God in the other, you will tear down every stronghold that hinders you. You will also be able to defeat every enemy that has been hiding inside it, including the strong man, the spirit of fear that has been protecting the door and not allowing you to go in and your blessings to come out!

Binding the Strong Man

Jesus said that you cannot go into the strong man's house and carry off with his possessions unless you first bind him. Jesus does not mention killing the strong man, only binding him. The reason why is that there are enemies you fight for a season and enemies that will continue to try to take you down throughout your entire life.

Take David and Goliath as an example. Goliath was an imposing figure yet David was able to kill him. David wanted to ensure he would never see that giant again so he cut off his head. In the same way, you will have the ability to defeat some of your giants, some of those flaws that try to keep you away from the presence of God. I have seen this in people that have had a drug addiction and have overcome it in such a way that it is no longer a temptation.

But you'll also encounters other enemies that you can't kill but you can bind. You can't put them in the grave, but you can stop them in their tracks. That is your assignment against the strong man, the Spirit of Fear.

Some may ask if God has given us the victory, why can't I cut the head off of the Spirit of Fear? It's important to know that Fear, isn't your everyday, run of the mill spirit. Remember, when Adam first sinned, even before God passed judgment on him in the Garden of Eden, he had realized he was naked and hid in fear. Fear has been around since the first days of humankind. It doesn't live in one place, nor does it just affect one area of your life. Fear is mobile, agile, and it disguises itself like a chameleon. You will win battles upon battles against fear, but the war never ends. Once you beat Fear in a certain area in your life, it rears its ugly head in another.

In 2 Corinthians 12, Paul wrote about the thorn in his side that he asked God to take away. God answered, "My grace is sufficient for you. My powers are made perfect in your weakness." Fear is like that thorn in our sides. If we lived a life devoid of fear, our ego's, our puffed up opinions of ourselves would cause us to drift away from God. However, being that God is omnipotent, the weapon of fear that the enemy tries to use to paralyze us, to stunt our growth and keep us inactive, God uses so that we may keep in contact with him. God has channeled the very power of fear and uses it in a way that shows off His power and glory. But it's important to understand that there is a difference between fear and the spirit of fear.

You must learn the art of binding the strong man of the Spirit of Fear in order to reach your full potential in God. Whenever God gives you the man or woman that you will spend the rest of your life with, the Spirit of Fear will show up to try to rob you of the blessing and promise destined in your marriage and through your legacy. Whenever doors start opening for you to fulfill your calling and the ministry that God has placed inside of you, the Spirit of Fear will rise to accuse you: "Who do you think you are? Have you forgotten what you've done? You know you don't have the ability to accomplish that!"

The Spirit of Fear

The problem for many Christians is that they surround themselves with people that can't recognize when the Spirit of Fear has entered the equation. People that don't know God can't sense its presence, they can't tell the telltale signs a mature Christian can, and they certainly don't speak courage and life into a situation. So the only voice a Christian surrounded by the wrong people hears, at times, is the voice of Fear, and sometimes the voices of his running mates, Doubt, and Feelings of Inadequacy.

But when you surround yourself with those who have eyes to see and ears to hear, they notice when the Spirit of Fear is trying to speak death into your ministry, marriage, and life. They recognize the symptoms and more importantly, they know who has the answers. They know how to bind the strong man and also how to put a muzzle over his mouth!

The Spirit of Fear is stronger than the Spirit of Darkness. Both spirits can manipulate you and blind you, but there's a difference. We are the Light of the world, and when the light shows up, the darkness vanishes. With the darkness gone, we see the path we need to take and many of us get on that path. However, Fear has a paralyzing agent that keeps people frozen. Even though they can see the way we have to go, even though they see the steps they need to take, they still don't move.

---

*Fear is so powerful and conniving
that it makes us teachers of it*

Fear has kept people at the same jobs their entire lives. Fear has kept people in the same town their entire lives. It has kept people's education levels the same ever since they quit school. It's kept a good man from asking a good woman to marry and him and later in life forced him to settle with someone of an unequal yoke.

Fear is so powerful and conniving that it makes us teachers of it and uses us as its puppets. Through our example, we have taught our children that we are only what our society tells us we are. Our children have seen us shy away from going into ministry, from going back to school as adults, from starting our own businesses, and unknowingly, we have spread fear into the hearts of our children.

The reason why the spirit of fear is so powerful and successful in people's lives is because it attacks in extremely sophisticated ways. It takes true events; our own memories, things we accept as factual happenings and distorts them. It keeps just enough truth in our thoughts to make it believable but hidden in those truths are lies, misconceptions, and false perceptions.

It's Time

As I stated before, the Spirit of Fear has been around for as long as the human species. It has convinced hundreds of billions of people throughout the history of humankind to believe its debilitating lies. As powerful as it is, it's got its kryptonite, we call him Christ Jesus, our risen savior. And in the name of Jesus, I speak to you Spirit of Fear, and I call you and tell you with all the authority given to me by the Spirit of God, "Fear. No more!" Your voice, in my life and in the lives of those who are reading this book, shall be heard no more!

Now, please allow me to me speak directly to you, dear reader: Don't let the enemy and the Spirit of Fear tell you what to do with the situations and circumstances that you have been through.

Take the very weapons the enemy has been using to keep you down and use them against them. The enemy has always thrown your past in your face to stop you from advancing but it's time for you to take hold of the pen and write the next chapter to your story. Gather your courage in Christ Jesus, the one who said your sins are forgiven and remember that our God who loves you so much said that he took your past, the very things the enemy uses, and threw them in the bottom of the ocean. Fear has people living a life of regret and shame because of something they have done but the truth is that God has forgiven you and doesn't even remember it! All you have to do is believe that and you can be FREE! Destroy the strongholds of your life, scatter the demons and principalities that have held you captive, and take back every promise the enemy has robbed you of.

It's time to stop running from your past. It's time to stop running from the mistakes you've made. It's time you stop running from your insecurities. It is now time for you to turn into a master blacksmith. And just like a blacksmith takes the steel and iron and melts it over the heat of the fire and begins to hit it with the hammer to mold into a sharp two-edged sword, it's time you take all your circumstances, all your mistakes, and all your downfalls, and put them over the fire of the Holy Spirit of God. Let the hammer of the word of God mold your past into a powerful weapon of spiritual warfare.

Declare it today: The voice of the spirit of fear will no longer be the primary voice that affects or defines me!

Inside the strongholds, yes, there are demons and generational curses and principalities and powers that have been trying to control and dominate your life. But remember, your future is also in there, as is your calling. Your freedom and your deliverance are in there as well. And the time has come to pick up your weapons of warfare, to pick up that big ole cross and use it like a sword, and get what the devil stole from you!

For many years you have watched, helplessly, as the enemy stole everything from you, one dream at a time, and hid them behind strongholds while the strongman stood guard. Now, it is the enemy's turn to sit and watch, helplessly, as you repossess everything back through the power of the blood of Christ Jesus. In the place of that kingdom that had enslaved you for years, drive mind-numbing spiritual terror into the Spirit of Fear. Let it bear witness to you, who was once a slave to its lies establishing the kingdom of God in the place where once his kingdom stood. You won't even have to tell it anything, it'll know that the King of Kings has arrived. Praise the Lord!

Chapter 3

The Seed Principle

What kind of God would allow other people's choices to affect another person's wellbeing?

To answer this question, and any other question about God, it's best if we see His heart by finding the answers in His word.

The Seed Principle

When God teaches on blessings and curses, in his word, He always teaches on how a person will be blessed in spite of himself. We see, often, that when God would bless or curse a person, the blessing or curse would also be upon their children and their children's children. That's because when God sees us, he doesn't only see us, he also sees a seed.

When God looks at us he sees a seed and everything destined to come out of that seed. When God first created the plants, he created in them the seeds that, once they die, would grow other plants of the same kind. When God sees you, He doesn't only see you. But He also sees your father, your grandfather, your great-grandfather, your son, your grandson, your great-grandson, etc. I pray you receive this powerful revelation!

Understand that this is the principle of the spirit realm. Do you think that when the devil tempted Adam to fall he was only looking at Adam? No. His mission was not to merely contaminate Adam but to also contaminate the seed that was within Adam.

We must be very careful what we speak in front of, and into our children. We must make sure that we are not being used as an instrument of the enemy to create strongholds within our children that they will have to deal with when they become adults. I mention this because many times as believers we tend to only deal with sins, bad choices, transgressions that only we commit. Not understanding that there could be strongholds we have to struggle against that didn't stem from something we did.

There are times when we are witnesses to an occasion, not active participants in it, just witnesses to it that leave us deeply scarred. You might think that this may never have happened to you. However, if you've ever seen something and said to yourself, "this will never happen to me!" then you too have been scarred by something someone else did.

Pastor Rod Carpenter said something I found to be very powerful. He says that life is lived in seasons but experienced in moments. I believe this to be true. Unfortunately for many, the enemy also knows and understands this concept.

In my house

When I was a teenager, I remember my father coming home from work looking like he needed a bed, a pillow, and a blanket. At the time, my mother had become obese. She weighed approximately 300 pounds. The minute my dad would attempt to sit down, I would hear my mom scream out to him, "Paquito!" As tired as he was, he would get up and go to the bedroom where she would be laying down, watching television. She would call him to the room to then ask him to get her water or something to drink. My father wouldn't complain or get into an argument with her. On the contrary, he would just get the cup of water, bring it, and ask her if she needed anything else. This routine began to make me angry.

"Paquito!"

I couldn't understand why, if he had been working so hard all day and she had been resting all day, she wasn't serving him. I would also hear the way she would speak to him. She would constantly scream at him or, when not screaming, talk to him in a tone I felt was disrespectful. But my dad would just go about helping my mom in just about every way she asked without complaining.

I felt like he wasn't receiving the honor he deserved. At times I felt as if it was worse than not being honored, at times I felt he was being abused. But he never complained. Nor did he ever mention that he felt like he was being abused or taken advantage of. He also never pulled me aside to explain why he allowed his wife to treat him in that manner. Because of this, rather than me becoming bitter towards my mother, without realizing, I began to develop resentment towards my father. The sad thing about this is that I didn't come to this understanding and revelation until I was fully-grown, married, with six children, and a pastor.

During my years of living with my parents, I remember going to bed many times and telling myself, "I will never allow a woman to speak to me in that manner." During that time, at about the age of 14 years old, I was introduced to the world of pornography. I had not realized it then, but the enemy was using the events that were happening in my mother and my father's marriage to get me addicted to porn.

Now that I'm more spiritually mature, I understand that one of the main reasons why I was so attracted to pornography was because of the dominance that the males had over the females in those disgusting and perverse movies. As a young Hispanic male who came from a culture of machismo and men proudly stated that they were the heads of the houses, watching the way my mother appeared to rule my father was a reality I had a tough time fathoming. The acts of pornography seemed right to me because again, the males dominated, the way my culture told me things should be. Getting caught up in porn made me even angrier towards the treatment of my father in my parent's marriage.

The enemy's plan was to set me up for failure when it came time for me to get married. He wanted to create strongholds in my life through events I was not a direct participant of, but a spectator to. So when I went to grasp the blessing of the merits that the Lord had for me, I would either reject it or be afraid to walk in it because of the spirit of fear.

I know now that the men who try to lord over their wives, who are chauvinistic, who need to always have the last word, are insecure. Some hide their insecurities behind the fact that they're physically stronger than the women they are with, while others hide behind some bible verses. The truth is that those men feel inadequate in many areas and by forcing their wives to submit to them is the only time they feel powerful. It's sad really.

But, I'm the Man of the House!

My fear was that my wife would rule me and that people would think of me less of a man like subconsciously, I thought of my father as a husband. I was determined to never let a woman, any woman, treat me like that, especially not my wife!

My fear and the addiction to pornography created in me a false narrative of what my marriage was going to be like, in and out of the bedroom. In my mind's eye, I had a clear vision of how my wife was going to act, how she was going to speak to me, how she was going to understand the way I expected her to behave, what she was going to do for me and how she was going to serve me.

What I hadn't realized was the vision I had was a distorted view of marriage based on years of porn addiction and bitterness. My definition of intimacy, respect, love, and to-death-do-us-part was created from the depths of a stronghold I had allowed to be built within my soul. I had no idea I was a prime candidate to have a dysfunctional marriage. Not only did I think I knew what to do, I also thought I knew what not to do.

Here's an interesting note regarding strongholds, they don't materialize in your spirit fully functional and complete. I entered into my marriage with a stronghold that had a solid, well-entrenched base. However, it had a lot of empty space of storage. That space typically gets filled with our concepts of being mistreated, misspoken to, ignored, or worse yet for me, disrespected.

The first few years of marriage - reality - and my chauvinistic perception of what marriage is supposed to be, clashed big time! I brought spirits of anger and pride into it on my own accord, but little did I know I also brought in an evil little scribe, someone that noticed and jotted down each

MUJER VIRTUOSA,

Porque su estima sobrepasa largamente a la de LAS PIEDRAS PRECIOSAS.

El corazón de su marido está en ella confiado, y no carecerá de ganancias.

Le da ella bien y no mal todos lo días de su vida

Busca lana y lino, y con voluntad trabaja con sus manos.

Es como nave de mercader; trae su pan de lejos.

Se levanta aún de noche y da comida a su familia y ración a su criadas.

Considera la heredad, y la compr y planta viña del fruto de sus mano

Ciñe de fuerzas sus lomos, y esfuerza sus brazos.

Ve que van bien sus negocios; su lámpara no se apaga de noch Aplica su mano al huso, y sus mano a la rueca.

MUJER VIRTUOSA,

MUJER VIRTUOSA...

ga su mano al pobre, y extiende sus manos al menesteroso.

tiene temor de la nieve por su ...ilia, porque toda su familia está vestida de ropas dobles.

a se hace tapices; de lino fino y púrpura es su vestido.

...arido es conocido en las puertas, ...ndo se sienta con los ancianos de la tierra.

...ce telas y vende, y da cintas al mercader.

...erza y honor son su vestidura; y se ríe de lo porvenir.

Abre su boca con sabiduría, y ...y de clemencia está en su lengua.

...sidera los caminos de su casa, y no come el pan de balde.

...e levantan sus hijos y la llaman bienaventurada; / su marido también la alaba:

...chas mujeres hicieron el bien; mas tú sobrepasas a todas.

...GAÑOSA ES LA GRACIA Y VANA HERMOSURA; LA MUJER QUE TEME AL SEÑOR, ESA SERÁ ALABADA.

...adle del fruto de sus manos, y ...enla en las puertas sus hechos.
PROVERBIOS 31:10-31

and every time I felt that my wife wasn't acting like the perfectly submissive wife I had envisioned. I began to feel disrespected or not honored as much as I thought I should have been.

The evil little scribe started to fill the empty space in the stronghold with the dangerously destructive feeling of discontentment. Mind you, my wife was amazing from the start. However, pornography and my misconception of marriage didn't allow me to appreciate everything she brought to our marriage.

Unknowingly, at times I would have feelings of joy and love in my marriage that brought me to the doors of the stronghold, ready to tear it down, only to realize the spirit of fear guarded it. A spirit that I was unequipped to fight with because I wasn't ready to accept who I really was.

Lamentably, still wrapped up in pornography, at the age of 23 I committed adultery against my beautiful wife and sinned against God. I remember clearly that on that very night, evil spirits attacked me. While my wife slept, I threw myself on top of a table we had in the middle of the living room. Lying on my back, I saw four or five different spirit beings (demons) flying over me. As I watched in sheer terror, they drifted closer and closer to me. One of them then went to touch me but disappeared, going through me, only to reemerge behind me. Then the other spirits started to fly in and out of my body in a diabolical frenzy.

"You have rebuked us and had cast us out through the years of your youth, but now you can do nothing to stop us."

My indiscretion had appeared to open a doorway in the spirit realm and I felt that the demons of lust and infidelity were trying to find a home in a stronghold within me. I had already felt repentant for my actions of earlier in the night but didn't know how to combat those spirits. I hastily went to my room and woke up my wife and explained to her the attack I was under.

"I had only seen this when there were infidelity issues," she said.

I somehow convince her to take her focus away from what she thought was the reason I was feeling the way I was and got her to get up and pray over me.

Strongholds in my life had been storing up all these things and because I didn't deal with any of it, I had now committed an act in which I had given the ability to the enemy to take everything from me.

As of this writing, I am 37 years old and have been forgiven not only by God but also my wife. We have been married for 17 years. By 2016, I had dealt and faced and conquered most, if not all, of the demons in which I had allowed to take control of my life. Or so, I thought.

Chapter 4

The Conference That Changed Everything

Pastor Ron Carpenter has been a mentor to me since the year 2000. Now, I have never had the privilege of shaking his hand, being that we've never met. However, through his teachings, whether he knew it or not, he had mentored me from afar.

My wife and I found out that Pastor Carpenter was presiding over a marriage conference in February of 2016. As we discussed whether we should go or not, I told her that I believed this conference, from someone I considered a spiritual mentor, is what our marriage needed to reach its full potential.

Now, those were the words that came out of my mouth. What I thought was slightly different. In my mind, I believed my wife really needed a breakthrough in order for our marriage to get to a higher level. She agreed that we should go and we bought the plane tickets to Greenville, South Carolina.

The week before the conference, being the good husband I am, I began to carefully explain to God (in the disguise of prayer) that my wife needed a spiritual shifting in her life. I made it really easy for Him to do His job, I practically laid on his feet everything that He needed to work on in my wife and, in case he wanted to know my opinion, exactly how I thought He should do it.

As the date of our flight approached, the weather forecast didn't look good. A huge Nor'easter was headed our way. (A Nor'easter is a powerful storm that typically drops tons of snow accompanied by strong winds that loves to knock out electricity. They're typically in the North East of the U.S., and we live in Massachusetts) We started to monitor the flights headed out of Logan Airport and, to our dismay, noticed that many flights were being canceled. However, a decision hadn't been made regarding our flight, so for a little while, we kept an eye on it, realizing that at any moment it could have been canceled and we would not have made it to the conference. Not wanting to risk missing the conference, we called the airline, got credit for our purchase, and decided to drive down to Greenville.

My wife didn't have her license at the time so I drove the entire 17 hours to South Carolina. We had a pleasant trip, in agreement with one another that we had a divine appointment with the Holy Spirit.

When we arrived at the conference, I remember feeling a sense of safety, as if I had reached a haven, a place where I could finally be vulnerable. A place where I could take off the suit of being a pastor, the shoes of being a father, the responsibility and burden of being a husband, and the stress of just simply being a man. Little did I know that the next morning I was going to have an experience that I would never forget. One that would mark my life forever.

When we got to the morning session on the Saturday of the conference, Pastor Ron Carpenter began to speak about an experience he had with his wife. I will not get into details about his experience because that is his personal testimony to release to those he chooses. But I'll say that towards the end of his testimony he began to speak on something that began to rock the very core of my being. He addressed men in the room, and everything just shifted.

"There are things that your father has done to you that has affected you profoundly. It has impacted you so deeply, yet you've never dared to bring it up to him. It's not that you had a bad father, it has nothing to do with him being good or bad. I know God is talking to someone in this room."

He couldn't have been more right. God was talking directly to me. He was taking things from my upbringing, things I had never known I had suppressed for years, and telling me that now was the time to deal with it.

Pastor Ron said, "I know that you've admired your father, and many other people also have, and rightly so. However, there were things he has said to you and worst yet, things left unsaid that has created a chasm of pain and bitterness in your spirit."

He continued digging into the subconscious of my past and bringing it into my present. I felt as if the air vacated the room. I began to cry uncontrollably and had an intense urge to find an escape. I started contemplating jumping over chairs and pushing people just to get out of there. It was unlike anything I had ever experienced.

I have been ministering and preaching since I was 13 years old. God has been using me in deliverance for that amount of time also. I had been a witness to many manifestations and deliverances. I had seen things manifest from the spirit realm to the natural that would scare most people. Now, I wasn't foaming at the mouth, I didn't start speaking in a different tongue or voice, my eyes didn't roll back into my head, nor did I slither on the floor like a snake, however, I understood that a tremendous manifestation of deliverance was happening from within me. I didn't know how to handle it.

"I have to find a way out of here," I whispered loudly to my wife.

"What?" She asked. She was enjoying the service and probably assumed I was as well. "What are you talking about?"

I was either going to run or receive a breakthrough like never before

---

"I have to get out of this room," As soon as I said that, I understood in my spirit that I had a crucial decision to make; I was either going to run or receive a breakthrough like never before. I held onto the chair in front of me tightly, as if it was saving me from being swept away by a mighty wind.

I did all I could just to stand there.

Sometimes you don't have to cry - you have to stand.

Sometimes you don't have to pray - you just have to stand.

Sometimes you don't have to shout - you just have to stand.

Sometimes you can't manipulate things to go your way, you just have to stand.

Like Pastor Carpenter said that day, I know God is talking to somebody.

Sometimes you don't have to explain - you just have to stand.

Sometimes you don't need to worship - you just need to stand.

There comes a time in our faith-walk that we don't have to do anything but stand in the presence of God and allow His light to burn the darkness away from our past.

I wanted to leave, the tears were pouring out, I could barely breathe, but I stood there and softly said, "God, have your way with me, I'm yours."

Then Pastor Ron told us to write a letter to our fathers. For a moment, I didn't think he was talking to me, it was 2016 and my father had gone to be with the Lord in 2003. But then, with my eyes closed, I heard him say, "You need to write a letter to your father, even if he's no longer with us. Write him what's in your heart."

This is the letter I wrote for my father that emotional day, word for word, unedited:

First off, I miss you. I miss you and the way that I can hardly bare it. I don't remember the day you passed away because I won't be able to deal with it year in and year out. So I choose to celebrate you through your birthday and not your day of death. Why are you gone? You left me, and I don't know why you did and make sure to be here. Stop smoking! That's all you needed to do. I don't know what I'm doing, and all you left me with is a shadow that cast over me that I can't fill!

You let mom treat you like dirt. She spoke to you nasty, slam doors, and you let her treat you like a child. You let her kill you. You let her get her way all the time. Maybe you do things you were not physically able to do. Now, I don't have you. The kids don't have you. I don't like going to mom's house because you belong there, and you're not there. I needed your voice, your presence. I needed you. But you're gone. And now, I'm alone yearning for fatherhood which I can't find, can't trust that there isn't a hidden agenda. I make mistakes and I don't even know how to admit to them because I don't know if you made them and how you fixed them or if you even admitted they were mistakes. I have to imagine you in heaven being proud, and sometimes it's just not enough.

When I wrote the last words - sometimes it's just not enough - I fell to the ground in total surrender, with tears and snot falling to the floor. I was too enthralled with God to care. I began to feel things start to crumble inside of me and felt things I couldn't put into words leaving my inner man. I was experiencing full-blown deliverance. I was being released from emotions and the thought process that had hindered my marriage, my life, and my future. For the first time, I understood that my mother and father had a dynamic to their marriage that worked, not only for her but also for him!

I realized that my mother made my father very, very happy. He loved her, he loved his children, he loved his job, and he loved his church. I remembered the smile on his face when we would speak and I remembered that he loved me, more than I ever realized. But through my bondage, I couldn't see it. But I saw my father through different eyes and realized that he loved his life.

My mother made my father very, very happy

The liberation I got from that understanding has allowed me to build a stronger relationship with my mother. Whenever I have a need that my mother can help me with, she's there to supply it. She's the primary caretaker of my grandmother, having dedicated the rest of her life to taking care of her mother. For the first time, I was able to see and appreciate the wonderful heart that my mother had. I was unable to see it or experience it while in bondage.

I wrote this story in this book for you to understand that there is nothing impossible for God. Many years after my father's death, Jesus visited me and freed me from a mind, from a perspective, that was flawed. He who the Son sets free is free indeed. I don't know what you need deliverance from, but I want you to know there is power in the blood of Jesus.

But it takes courage to be willing to change something that has taken root, which has built a stronghold in you for many years. It's also hard to acknowledge, at times because of pride, that somebody else's actions affected our character. But once the light of God shines upon our memories and skewed recollections, we are freed of guilt, shame, and misunderstandings.

As my wife and I had suspected, that marriage conference transformed our marriage. I was convinced that God was going to work on my wife but He had other plans. To know that my father loved his wife and loved his life made me loving mine easier. I've learned always to love when God's plans are done and not mine.

Chapter 5

My Father's the Pilot

"For God has not given us a spirit of fear..."
2 Timothy 1:7

In a letter written to Timothy, Paul writes and declares to Timothy, "for God has not given you a spirit of fear," This is a very powerful proclamation. Let's look at this statement, written by Paul, and inspired by the Holy Spirit:

The word 'fear' in the Greek is, "deilia," which means 'timidity.' This word comes from the root word, "deilos," which means faithless. The foundation of fear is faithlessness. This means that fear only enters when we live a life continuously losing faith in who Jesus Christ, our Lord and Savior, is. That's why Hebrew 11:6 says, " for he who comes to God must believe that He is, and that

He is a rewarder to those who diligently seek Him"
(Hebrews 11:6).

Fear keeps us from believing in who HE is. We
allow our past experiences to dictate what God can
and cannot do in our lives. It's not that we don't
necessarily believe in God. It's just that we don't
believe that God can do it, for us!

You see, the enemy understands how it works.
He knows that faith is the currency of heaven. Fear
robs us of that currency. The enemy fights so hard
to not let you forget your past because your fears
are connected to your past. The devil knows that
if you can get to the place of forgetting your past,
you will be equipped, by the Holy Spirit of God, to
conquer and obliterate your fears!

Paul is letting Timothy know that he does not
have a spirit of fear because he doesn't have a spirit
of faithlessness. Fear only comes in when we lose
faith in an ability, person, or thing, to protect us
or hold us up. The devil understands that he must
attack your faith in God, and rob you of it, in order
for the powerful weapon of fear to be activated
and create havoc and torment in your life. Where
there is faith, fear cannot accomplish the task it has
been sent out to do. With faith, no weapon formed
against you can prosper!

I believe that Paul understood this. I believe it's
why in Ephesians 6:16, Paul calls it "the shield of
faith." Paul makes a connection with the part of the
armor that is used to block incoming attacks, with

faith. Why? It's faith that blocks and keeps out attacks from the enemy, like fear.

A person without faith is like a soldier without a shield. He might be able to withstand some hits, but sooner or later one of those blows will penetrate the armor. When it does, the soldier feels as if his only option is to retreat. That is precisely what happens to a person who allows fear, through faithlessness, to enter the equation. It gets you to a place where you feel that the only option you have is to retreat and give up. The job of the spirit of fear is to paralyze you. To paralyze you in areas where you were meant to succeed and exceed.

The spirit of fear makes you afraid of heights in order for you not to climb. The spirit of fear makes you afraid of the dark so that you will be afraid of walking into places that have no light and for you to be the light. The spirit of fear has an assignment on your life to make you retreat before you can even get started. It bases its strategy on making you focus on what you can and cannot do. It tries to make you focus on your insecurities, weaknesses, lack of resources, lack of education, lack of self-esteem, and failures. Because based on these, your enemy is correct: you do not have what it takes to get it done. But this is only half of the truth. Because the word of God says in Zechariah 4:6, "not by might, nor by power, but by my Spirit, says the Lord of hosts."

It is a fact that you do not have enough to get it done. But the enemy has been trying to block the second, and most important part, of this truth.

That although you don't have what it takes, it's not based on what you can or can't do. It's based on the power and on the strength of the spirit of the Lord that lives within you. It's not based on your strength, but on His. It's not based on your power, but on His. It is not based on your intellect but on his wisdom.

Joel 3:10 says, "Let the weak say I am strong." Paul wrote in 2nd Corinthians 12:10, "therefore I take pleasure in infirmities, in reproaches, in necessities, in persecutions, in distress for Christ's sake: for when I am weak, then I am strong."

When I stop basing my walk on my strength and I come to the realization that I am too weak for the assignment I have been given I only have one place to turn to, my Father, my Lord and Savior Jesus Christ, and to the power and strength of the Holy Spirit of God. That's why Paul wrote in 2nd Corinthians 12:9, "and he said unto me, my grace is sufficient for you: for my strength is made perfect in weakness."

In the Greek, the word for strength is, *dunamis*. It's the same word Jesus used when he said, "but ye shall receive **power** - dunamis, after that the Holy Ghost comes upon you: and ye shall be witnesses unto me both in Jerusalem, and in all Judea, and in Samaria, and unto the uttermost part of the earth." It's interesting to note that this word, *dunamis*, is the root word from where we get the word dynamite.

Before the disciples get to the upper room and receive the Holy Ghost, in Acts chapter 2, they had first been confronted and defeated by fear. When the soldiers came for Jesus at the Mount of Olives, and after Peter cut off the ear of the soldier and Jesus picked it up and put it back in its place, the disciples ran and dispersed. They ran away because of fear. Peter denied Jesus because of fear. After Jesus resurrects, he finds them in a house hiding, locking all the doors, because of fear.

Peter denied Jesus because of fear

The resurrected Jesus re-gathers them and tells them that he's leaving but that the comforter (the Holy Spirit) is going to continue the work. He tells them to go to the upper room and wait for the pouring out of the Holy Spirit. He tells them that when this happens they will receive *dunamis*.

While there in the upper room, they receive the baptism of the Holy Ghost and begin to speak in languages they had never spoken before. The people that were around in the city began to hear the commotion. They gathered around and assumed that they must have been drunk. Peter then came out and began to preach to the multitude with courage.

He tells them the Christ that you crucified has resurrected and now calls you to repentance. 3,000 souls converted in that one sermon that Peter gave with courage. What happened to Peter? What happened to Peter that made him shift from a man full of fear who not only abandoned Jesus but denied him, to a person who courageously stood among the very people that screamed crucify him! Crucify him! And preached one of the greatest sermons ever recorded in the history of Christianity? It was the dunamis!

It was the Holy Spirit of God shifting Peter's spirit to understand that God's grace was sufficient and that the power of the Holy Ghost would perfect itself through Peter's weakness. He fully understood that it wasn't by his strength, as he thought it was when he took the sword and cut the soldiers ear off, but by the power of the Holy Spirit of God, which he let himself be guided by after he was baptized in the Holy Spirit. That revelation, that outpouring of dunamis, is why he was able to preach such a powerful message and have 3,000 souls come to the feet of Christ.

When Paul tells Timothy to "stir up the gift of God, which is by the putting on of hands," he's talking about the very Holy Ghost that fell upon the 120 people in the upper room. It activates all the gifts of the spirit God has given to us, to bring freedom and deliverance to ourselves, those around us, and those who are lost in the world. In essence, Paul is telling Timothy - the same gift of God that is in me is also in you, through the laying of my hands on you. So now your behavior towards trials and tribulations should duplicate mine

That's why it's very important that you filter, through the Holy Spirit and through the word of God, who you allow to pour into you. It's not wise to listen to just anyone when needing advice on your marriage. Not everyone is qualified to give you financial advice. The Bible says in Proverbs 15:31-33, "he whose ear listens to the life-giving reproof will draw among the wise. He who neglects discipline despises himself, but he who listens to reproof requires understanding. The fear of the Lord is the instruction for wisdom, and before honor comes humility."

Proverbs 24:6 declares, "for by wise guidance you will wage war, and in an abundance of counselors there is victory." Isn't it incredible that the wisest man to ever walk this earth knew that even he needed guidance and counseling? He understood that he couldn't just let anybody speak into his life.

There should be criteria for those who have the right to bring counseling and guidance to your life. They should be God-fearing people who pray and live at His feet, listening to what He has to say. They should be people whose daily diet consists of prayer, eating the word of God, and interceding for the saints and lost souls.

When many look for counseling, they have a bad habit of seeking fellowship and commonality, instead of correction, rebuke, and direction. In other words, we look for people that are going to agree that it's okay for us to be in the condition we find ourselves in. We want people to say,

"I get you, girl."

"I completely understand what you're going through."

"I would have done the same thing!"

"You're right, what other choice did you have?"

"Stay exactly the way that you are, don't change."

We fall into the trap of the blind leading the blind

We also tend to gravitate towards people that are basically in the same condition we're in. We fall into the trap of the blind leading the blind. The reason why so many people reject the teachings and sermons of pastors and evangelists who tell us we need to change is because we disqualify them by thinking that they're not in our shoes. When, in actuality, because they are not in our messed up state is precisely why we should listen to them!

Instead, we begin to question how they got there. More importantly, those who we've been trusting the teachers and preachers begin to question their guidance and convince themselves and others not to listen to them. We must understand that sorrow, bitterness, anger, and brokenness loves fellowship.

People who are in this condition love to find other people in the same condition, and speak into other people's lives to convince them, every day, to stay in that situation, like them. They do this because they don't want to be anything other than normal. So if they can convince enough people to be like them, they'll become part of the majority, thus making their condition one of normality.

> *I remember your true faith. It is the*
> *same faith your grandmother Lois had*
> *and your mother Eunice had.*
> *I am sure you have that same faith also.*

2 Timothy 1:5 (NLV)

Paul hits Timothy with the, "Do You Remember?" When I read this, a voice in my spirit said to me "son, everything is not meant to be forgotten." I started to understand that I needed to be guided by the Holy Spirit, so that He could show me the experiences, relationships, and encounters that had marked my life in such a negative way that they were left open the doors for fear to enter my life. At the same time, there were experiences, relationships, and encounters that had marked my life in such powerful and anointed ways that I was going to be able to go back and draw strength from them. WOW! My God! This changed my life forever.

It wasn't so much about forgetting what I have been through, but more about allowing the Holy Spirit to put it in the correct perspective. I began to understand that there was power in my pain. There was anointing being squeezed out through the crushing, and the pressing.

It meant for me also to remember who God has been in my life. To recall all the times I was in a valley, and he showed up. The many times he came and pulled me out of a living hell. You see, the spirit of fear tries to overwhelm you in such a way that it makes you forget who God is. Remember that you've been in bad situations before and God has never shown up too late. But the spirit of fear clouds our minds in a way in which while we are going through the storm, or confronting a giant, that we tend not to remember that we have faced and defeated those same types of giants before. You've experienced storms like this before and each and every time you've come out in one piece.

◆◆

Remember that you've been in bad situations before and God has never shown up too late

◆◆

The spirit of fear tries to make us forget. Forget the fact that we had been in dire situations before and that God had worked it out. Why is the devil hell-bent on making us forget? Because when we don't remember what worked, we begin to try to find new ways to work things out. We become desperate and operate under panic. Then things seem to speed up on us.

Who's Your Pilot?

There's a story about a great evangelist on an airplane one time when turbulence, like nothing he ever experienced, struck the plane. Instantly fear took hold of him, and by the sound of it, everyone else in the cabin. As the turbulence made the breathing masks fall in front of everyone's faces and people were screaming, some crying, he noticed a girl of about eleven years old. What caught his attention was that she wasn't scared. She was reading a book as if they're lives weren't in danger. If anything, she seemed annoyed with the jolting of the plane caused by the turbulence!

They made it through the storm and, once they were in the airport, the evangelist ran over to her and asked, "I've never seen bravery like that. How were you not scared?"

She looked at him and said, quite nonchalantly, "My father's the pilot." and walked away.

At first, the evangelist didn't know why her father being the pilot would stop her from being scared from the crazy turbulence. It was much later when the revelation dawned on him... the girl wasn't afraid because her father was the pilot. She must've taken many flights with her father at the helm. The first few times that she experienced turbulence, she probably got scared and cried to her father. But her father had explained this to her - "Daughter, you have to understand that the plane I have you on can fly over the winds and clouds that cause the storms that bring the turbulence."

The evangelist understood that the little girl wasn't scared because time and time again, regardless of how hard the rain struck the plane, regardless of how strong the winds blew against the plane, her father had brought her through the storms - sometimes by going through it and sometimes by going over it - over and over again.

In the same way, look back at the times you've called on God and you'll realize that every time, he has brought you through the storm. There's no reason to fear, regardless of the situation you find yourself in as you read this because your father is the pilot of your life and he will get you through whatever storm comes your way.

I understand that everything I had been through was not in vain. God was going to help me let go of those things and people that were withering my heart away. The Holy Spirit was not only going to reveal and expose those things that were making me bitter, but he was also going to obliterate them! But when it came to everything else I had encountered and endured, I was going to be able to remember who and what made me into the man of God I am today.

The Holy Spirit was going to bring to remembrance my spiritual parents, and how they taught me the importance of fasting and intercession. The Spirit of the Lord was going to bring to my memory those moments when I thought it was all over, but God showed up just in time to save me, and see me out. It is remembering who and what made me that I will draw the strength, power, authority, and anointing to overcome all my fears, through the love of God.

It's about remembering what is in me. This is the reason that I believe Paul tells Timothy, after reminding him of his mother and grandmother, "**I am persuaded that it is in thee also.**"

Chapter 6

Fear is an Antigen

Have you ever stopped to examine the times you've strayed away from God's will? More often than not, it was never based on just one decision during one circumstance. It was the enemy throwing different scenarios that you reacted badly to by making poor choices rather than seek the will of God. But it wasn't just one decision. It was various linked together that got you to fall and be in that pit-like condition. By the time you noticed what had happened, you realized how far you've gotten from God and how quickly you got there.

We'll say things like, "just the other day I was lifting my hands and worshipping with a smile on my face and peace in my heart. Now look at me. I'm depressed, confused, and don't know how to get out of this. How did I get here so quickly?"

The enemy's plan is for us to make a long-term decision during a temporary situation. He wants for the consequences of our actions to last much longer than the actual situation we are in when we make a hasty decision.

If you sit down and meditate, you realize that how you got there was through Satan throwing temptations and situations at you and you reacted from a state of desperation and panic. You got to the condition that you found yourself in through a chain of events that caused an adverse chain reaction. And we find ourselves behaving and talking differently than who God says we are.

We are made up of three beings: spirit, soul, and body. Understand that we have a responsibility of taking care of and managing all three parts that make up who we are. We cannot be all body or all spirit or all soul. You may have heard teachings instructing you to just concentrate on the spiritual and not worry about the other two. I believe, according to the word of God, that those lessons are incorrect.

Throughout the Bible we are instructed what and what not to eat (Proverbs 23:1-3, Daniel 1:8, 12, 13, 15, First Corinthians 6:12-13). It also speaks to us on how to make sure that we keep the soul healthy (3 John 1:2, Hebrews 10:22, Psalms 42:11). It even teaches us on how to keep the mind healthy (Matthew 22:37, Romans 12:2).

If I give all my attention to the spirit, I will have the glory and live in the glory. But by neglecting the body, I now have a spirit that's living in the glory but encased inside a body that doesn't have the strength to keep up with the glory that the spirit is living in. Remember that even though it is the spirit that we feed when we pray, if our body is breaking down, it will be very difficult for us to stay kneeling down or praying for long periods of time if our bodies are not in good shape.

I have known people that have an urgent desire and the ability to seek God deeply. But their physical bodies don't allow them to do so because they didn't take the time to stay in decent shape. I don't mean that you have to be a bodybuilder, a marathon runner, or have a body of a model. But you should take care of the temple of the Holy Ghost.

We can't take care of the spirit and the body and abandon the soul. Because then we'll have a spirit full of glory, a body healthy enough to hold that glory, but emotions in such an unstable state that we won't be able to minister that glory correctly nor be able to use the energy our bodies have and focus it in the right direction. God has called us to have a balance among all three.

The only thing is that we must live according to the spirit, meaning that we need to pay attention to all three but must allow the spirit to control the other two. In other words, every decision we make for and through our bodies, every emotion and every thought process that we allow in our soul, must be filtered and permitted by the spirit while it's submitted to the Spirit of God and the word of God.

Notice how Paul tells Timothy, "For I have not given you a Spirit of Fear. But of power, love, and a sound mind." He doesn't say a Spirit of Power, a Spirit of Love, and a Spirit of a Sound Mind. Because we only have one spirit. At one time I thought this verse was speaking about different spirits. But what God is saying, through Paul, is that the spirit I have given you does not have fear, as part of its DNA.

When the spirit of fornication attacks and gets a hold of someone, it infects the spirit of the person, which in turn makes the person commit an ungodly act through the body (the flesh). In other words, the name of your spirit doesn't change to the spirit of fear. What has happened is that the spirit of fear has come like a virus or infection, and now your spirit is contaminated.

For me to make my next point, I need to discuss a little bit of anatomy. I want us to get on the same page as to what an antigen is and what an antibody is.

Antigen: any substance that causes your immune system to produce antibodies against it.

Antibody: a protective protein produced by the immune system in response to the presence of a foreign substance, called an antigen.

So, an antigen is a sickness, an infection, a virus that attacks our bodies - little invaders that attack. When attacked, our bodies create a protein called an antibody (or immunoglobulin) to eradicate the antigen from the body. Are we all on the same page? Good, you're going to like this.

The spirit of fear acts like an antigen when it attacks a physical body. Like an antigen, it's a virus, a bacteria that wants to spread through your whole spirit, reach your soul, and invade your body. Ecclesiastes 12:7 declares, "then shall the dust return to the earth as it was: and the spirit shall return unto God who gave it."

Fear is afraid of God

God does not understand the meaning of fear. He doesn't know what it is to be afraid of anything. The creator will never be scared of the creation. If anything, fear is afraid of God.

The Bible declares that the spirit will go back to from where it came from, which is to God. As fear is foreign to God, it is also foreign to our spirit. When an antigen is present and attacking a body, the way to defeat it, your body creates anti-bodies to fight against the antigen. Antibodies are blood proteins produced in response to and counteracting a specific antigen. Antibodies aren't there all the time. God has created us in a way that they are produced when the body detects something alien, such as bacteria or viruses. The antibodies bind the antigen and shut it off. This is the natural process the body has been designed with in order to take back control from invaders.

God's spirit with us acts like an antibody, equipped to combat any virus or bacteria that wants to invade it.

These are the gifts of the spirit found in Galatians 5:22-23; love, joy, peace, forbearance, kindness, goodness, faithfulness, gentleness, and self-control. These fruits of the Spirit are the antibodies that it contains within. When your spirit can't produce this antibody, that's when that virus, called the spirit of fear, comes in and infects every part of who we are. But when we have the antibodies, made by the fruits of the Spirit, it clashes against fear. If fear is virus, the cure is having the fruits of the Spirit.

No one likes to feel afraid, it's a horrible, debilitating feeling. Many believers wonder, if this feeling is so bad, why does God allow the spirit of fear to attack us? You have to understand that when we're attacked is when we realize we need Him and that we can't find the cure on our own. But when we surrender to Him, and we seek to truly know Him, we get filled with the fruits of the spirit, which takes that fear and turns a scenario doomed for failure into a success.

God loves to have a personal relationship with every human being, and for every human to give Him glory. When we are afraid, we seek a closer relationship with Him and He gets the glory when we are able to overcome the fear.

When the fear antigen comes and attacks your spirit, it awakens the antibodies (fruits of the spirit), and powerful weapons such as faithfulness, self-control, and peace, a unique peace that goes beyond human understanding, and they defeat it.

Boldly proclaim Romans 8:37, "But we have power over all these things through Jesus who loves us so much!"

Call on 1 John 4:4, "... the one who lives in you is stronger than the one who is in the world."

You have the cure for the foreign substance called fear that has been trying to invade your spirit, and your mind, to paralyze you. Just remember who you are. Remember what's inside you. Remember who you got it from. Do as Paul told Timothy to do: stir up the gift of God, it's in you!

Chapter 7

Your Destiny is Too Big

When children learn how to ride a bike, they usually start with training wheels on the back tire put on by the parents. These training wheels allow them to learn the basics of riding a bike; how to use coordination to pedal, control the bicycle, and guide it to where they want to go. Once they get to the point where they feel they've have mastered riding with training wheels, they ask their parents to take them off.

The parents take the training wheels off, but when the child begins to ride, they don't let go of the bike. They hold on to and run with the bike until they feel that the bike is steady enough that the child can control the bike and not fall. As the child is riding on his or her own, the parents begin shouting out instructions such as, "Keep looking straight! Keep the steering steady! You got this!"

We live in a time where nobody wants or feels as if they need correction

---

The parents are reminding the child what they learned in training. In the same way, this is the job of our spiritual parents. It's their job to train us up in the ways of the Lord, and then remind us to activate what we learned during our training - to best handle those moments of trials, tribulations, temptations, and turmoil.

We are living in a time referred to as the Fatherless Generation. We hear more about broken homes, single families, children with fathers in prison, abortion being accepted by the mainstream, abusive husbands and abusive wives, and the feminist movement, than in any other generation in human history. I truly believe that this "fatherlessness" or "parentless-ness" epidemic and mentality has seeped into the church and Christian culture. It seems as if we live in a time where nobody wants or feels as if they need correction, rebuke, or direction. People simply want to come to church on Sundays, leave their tithes (if they feel like it), sing a couple of songs, hear a 15-minute thought from the Pastor, and continue about their business.

Your destiny is too big to be playing these games!

I remember growing up in church and having 2 or 3 spiritual mothers. There was a lack of spiritual fatherhood back then as well. But my spiritual mothers, and aunts, had the authority to smack me upside my head, and pull me to the pulpit and reprimand me, "What are you doing playing with God, boy? You know your purpose is too big for you to be playing these games!"

After that, they would lead me to the throne of God to pull me out of my sin. They wouldn't let up until I got my breakthrough. My biological mom would be right in the back, with her arms extended in my direction, declaring that I get my deliverance.

This type of spiritual parenting is what's missing in today's church. For some reason, the church believes that as the world trends and ways change, the church should change also. I believe that for the church to stay relevant to this generation, we can't stay stuck in our ways. But there are biblical, foundational truths that surpass and supersede every generational boundary. Music styles may change, but the message in the lyrics and the anointing in the sound should not. Dress styles may vary, but the moderation should not. Technology and social interaction may change, but the way to seek God's face should not. Popular church trends should never replace God's tried and true ways on how to enter into his presence, to his throne room, which is through fasting, prayer, vigil, reading His Word, and a continuous seeking of God's face and will.

Children need an identity

God has given my wife and me the honor and privilege of pastoring a church that is full of people whose family, community, and even society, had given up on. We are privileged to pastor ex-convicts, former drug dealers, drug addicts, and alcoholics who have been redeemed by the blood of the Lamb, transformed by the power of the Holy Spirit, and have been adopted by The Father. At first glance, it didn't make any sense that God had chosen me to pastor this kind of church. My wife had come from a very rough childhood, where she had experienced a drug-dealing father who was abusive to her mother and had lived a life in and out of prison. I, on the other hand, had experienced, "Mr. Rogers' neighborhood" in the middle of Harlem, NY.

Don't get me wrong. I grew up in a very rough neighborhood. I remember playing in the schoolyard during recess and seeing little crack bottles on the floor. There was always some sort of police presence around my street. There was always a killing, robbery, or drug bust happening. But somehow, my parents managed to build a peaceful, respectful, loving, family-oriented, home. I can't remember my father ever saying a cuss word (he probably said many before getting saved). I never saw a verbal or physical altercation between my parents.

It makes sense to me that the Lord chose me my wife because I feel she has the ability to identify with those that had come from rough upbringings and tough childhoods.

When we knew we were going to become pastors, I assumed that our church was going to be populated mainly by women and children. I was shocked to see the types of people that came to our church, and a little at a loss. I felt out of place. I thought, how could I, having come from a loving, nurturing home with two parents who cared for my physical body and spiritual soul, identify with men that had come from a fatherless childhood? How could I minister to people if I couldn't look them in the eye and say, "I understand. I've been there."

One night, I heard the voice of the Spirit, speak to me. That's the voice that doesn't use audible words. It just drops a message in your spirit. It's that voice that, without syllables, words, or sentences, can speak to the most profound places in your heart and soul. I heard THAT voice say to me, "son, I didn't send you for you to identify with them, but for them to identify with you."

I realized that they didn't need me to understand them, that in the big scheme of things, they didn't care if I did or not. They needed to learn how to live a Godly life. They needed to know they were forgiven. They needed to know they were loved. They needed to see a husband treat his wife right. They needed to witness a father love on his children.

Some of them had never seen that, they were craving it without even knowing they were. God had plans of saving their families, and He knew they needed to see a Christian man, although flawed, do his best to live according to His word. God let me know that He brought them to me because of the work He had done in me.

I want you to understand this in your spirit — God only wants good things for you. However, whether in or out of the will of God, we will go through trials and tribulations. Those things that the enemy tries to use to destroy our relationships, our finances, our health, our mindset, and our status in the community, God uses them for good if we give them to Him.

God will then use that test and bring forth our testimony. God will take that mess that we came from and form our message. We will be equipped to speak life to others in similar situations that we've been through. However, it doesn't have to be that way. You can never do time in jail and speak life to a life-long prisoner. You can be Puerto Rican and speak life to an Asian. You can be rich and speak life to a beggar. You can be living paycheck to paycheck and speak life to a millionaire. You can be sick and speak life to a healthy marathon runner. There is no one, regardless of his or her religion, social status, height, weight, age, marital status, sexual orientation, or race that God can't use you to speak the power of the gospel to. No one.

When that Word was dropped in my spirit, it immediately brought me back, in the form of a flashback, to my childhood and my upbringing. I understood that it was all God's plan. He had orchestrated the entire thing. Being raised in the hood, but given to parents that would never allow the hood to raise me. God had ordained my parents to shield me from the drugs, alcohol, crime, death, and criminal mentality I was subjected to every day. My surroundings were like hell, but my home, my cave, my bunker, was Heaven on earth, or as close as it could be while living in the ghetto.

God had set it up in a way where I could, as a spiritual father, understand the people in my church and empathize with them, even though we didn't share similar pasts. I was so worried about identifying with them, and the whole time, God's plan was to get them to identify with something and someone so that they could say, "I know that right now I have an identity, a lineage, that has tried to name me, claim me, and give me my name, but I no longer want to be connected to that lineage, I want to be adopted and made a son or daughter of the lineage of Christ."

By the grace, mercy, and calling of God, my wife and I have been used by God to pull men, women, and young people out of the debilitating history of drug addiction, prison, divorce, broken relationships, gangs, and prostitution, and into a genealogy of peace, fullness, joy, purpose, healing, power, authority, and anointing, through Jesus Christ! This can only come about when men and women find their identity.

But the spirit of fear will get us to such a place that we believe that the only identity that we can have is the current one in which we live. But identity can only come from parenthood. Remember that the Bible says in 2nd Corinthians 5:17, "Therefore if any man be in Christ, he is a new creature: old things are passed away; behold, all things are become new."

This includes your birthplace and who gave birth to you. When Nicodemus asked Jesus, "how am I to be born again? How can I re-enter my mother's womb to be born a second time?" Jesus answered, "Except a man be born of water and of the spirit, he cannot enter into the kingdom of God."

Notice how Jesus mentions two things (the water and the Spirit) in describing a second birth. We are taught in biology class that the first process in our creation was when daddy's sperm entered mommy's egg. Just like you need two items to conceive a baby in the physical world, two items are necessary for us to be born again in the supernatural.

Now, God connects us with spiritual parents, who are connected to God and used by God to bring us to complete spiritual maturity. They help us, not only walk in the fullness of what God has promised us but also to be able to manage it correctly, according to the word of God. Does this mean that we are to forget or disregard our earthly parents? No, not by any means.

God gave our earthly parents to us, or better yet, God gave us to them, for them to nurture us physically and emotionally, and lead us in the right direction spiritually. But there are many occasions in which earthly parents have not been able to lead their earthly children into, not only salvation but into the very destiny God had designed for them. So when we are born again, God, in his infinite wisdom, connects us to mentors and spiritual parents. They guide us, teach us to stay humble, teach us how to serve, keep the passion burning inside of us to seek holiness, and show us how to consecrate ourselves for the Lord's purposes.

Chapter 8

This is Who You Are

"Now I say, that the heir, as long as he is a child, differs with nothing from a servant, though he be Lord of all; but is on the tutors and governors onto the time appointed of the father."

Galatians 4:1-2

I feel led to remind you that this is who you are. I prophesy over you, dear reader, you are no longer that weak-minded person whose mind gets changed by popular opinion. You are no longer that unsteady person that the waves can topple, even when the sand underneath your feet shifts. You are no longer a sapling but a mighty palm tree that bends in the face of the mightiest winds but doesn't break. You are no longer that person who is dominated by carnal desires. You are no longer that person that your enemy said you are. You are no longer the person someone cursed you to be. You are no longer that person you never wanted to be. See, the old you would go cry in a corner with tears streaming down crying, "I can't take this anymore. I give up!"

The new you, the reborn you, is the type of person who, even in the midst of a storm, even as tears roll down, screams rebelliously at the spirit of fear, "My tears are evidence that I'm hurting, but it's also letting me know that I'm still alive. I ain't dead yet and this fight ain't over!"

And even though tears are visible on my face, I will proclaim the entirety of Psalms 121, which states,

---

You are no longer that unsteady person that the waves can topple

---

"I will lift up my eyes to the hills, from where my help comes from. My help comes from the Lord, who made heaven and earth.

He will not suffer my foot to be moved: he that keeps me will not slumber. Behold, He who keeps Israel shall neither slumber nor sleep. The Lord is my keeper: the Lord is my shade upon my right hand. The sun shall not smite me by day, nor the moon by night.

The Lord shall preserve me from all evil: he shall preserve my soul. The Lord shall preserve my coming and going from this time forth, from now till the end of time."

You are a new creature. That means that everything about you was made new. That includes your mind, your emotions, the way you process situations, and the way you confront them. You no longer will operate from a state of panic or desperation. Under the anointing of the Holy Spirit, you will be cool, calm, and collected. No longer will the spirit of fear be able to speed up time and make you feel like things are moving too fast. Everybody around you might start panicking, but you'll see things in slow motion. You will be able to process your environment, and under the guidance of the Holy Spirit of God make correct, Godly decisions. And from now on, you don't get moved or swayed. You only move when God says so. That's the new you!

Paul then tells Timothy in 2nd Timothy 1:6, "Therefore I remind you to stir up the gift of God which is in you through the laying on of hands."

Paul paid a heavy price for the glory that was over his life. He had been beaten, bruised, falsely accused, imprisoned, shipwrecked, and persecuted to have the level of glory and anointing that was over his life. He tells Timothy that the gift of God in which he had paid a very high price for, was placed inside of Timothy, by the laying of Paul's hands over him.

In other words, Timothy did not have to go through the pain that Paul did to receive the glory that Paul had. You see, Timothy, at that moment, felt like he didn't have the strength to keep going. But the glory that was within him, the anointing that flew inside of him, originated from his grandmother, his mother, and from his spiritual father, Paul.

He goes on to tell Timothy, "For God has not given us the spirit of fear; but of power, and of love, and of a sound mind." Paul could proclaim this with certainty because what was in Timothy was an extension of what was already in him. And Paul was 100% sure of what was in him was the spirit of power, of love, and of a sound mind.

Chapter 9

Just walk on water

As God's children, we need to make sure we possess the gift of discernment. To tell the difference between when God is speaking to us and when the enemy is trying to deceive us. The Bible says in John 10:27, "My sheep hear my voice, and I know them, and they follow me."

The gift of discernment is critical to defeating the spirit of fear and to not getting sidetracked away from following the direction that God wants to take us in. This is important because what can be a blessing from God in one season can be a trap of the enemy in another. In one season, a job could be a blessing God has sent for you to be able to sustain you and your family. In another season, that same job can be an instrument of the enemy to stand in your way from reaching your career or becoming a business owner. You see, it's the same job having a different assignment, depending on what season you are in.

In Matthew 14:24-32, we find the disciples on a ship in the midst of the sea. They're caught in a severe storm, and the winds and waves are tossing their boat about. Jesus is not with them, he had gone up into a mountain to pray. During the fourth watch, Jesus began walking towards them, yes, you know the story, when he walked on water.

The fourth watch is between 3 AM and 6 AM. It's the time of night just before dawn, right before the sun rises. It's also the darkest time of night. Verse 26 says, "When the disciples saw him walking on the sea, they were troubled, saying, it's a spirit; and they cried out for **fear.**"

What can be a blessing from God in one season can be a trap of the enemy in another

---

These men, his disciples, had cried out in fear. The same men who had been following Jesus, hearing him preach, witnessing the powerful miracles God did at his hands, they were practically living with him. Yet, they didn't recognize that the man walking on water was their master.

Fear will rob you of your vision

The spirit of fear will not allow you to see God in your situation even though He's not only there, but has been since the beginning. Because of fear, the disciples could not tell what was of God what wasn't.

The enemy will never show up in your life and come right out and introduce himself to you, "Hi. I'm Satan." He will never show up and, before attacking you, announce claim responsibility for what's about to happen.

One of the main strategies the enemy uses is creating various situations of turmoil in your life. While you're focused on managing those situations, he launches another attack, this one directly to the place he wanted to attack all along. His attacks are so diverted that you don't realize you're under a strategic attack from the enemy.

Imagine the situations of turmoil as weather fronts. Those of us who know a little about weather forecasting understand that storms are created when two or more fronts crash into one another. This is how "Mother Nature" creates storms and hurricanes. In this same fashion, the enemy creates all these different situations in order for them to crash into each other to create storms in your life. That's when the spirit of fear attacks and begins to make us feel like we're not only stuck in the storm but that we're going to die in it.

Once we're caught up in the storm and operating under the spirit of fear, our vision gets clouded. We can't tell if the movement is of God or if the enemy is manipulating events. When it's God, we think it's from the devil, and when it's of the devil, we think it's of God. When our vision is blurred, it's easy to be confused. Similar to how the disciples found themselves.

There's another story in the Bible where Jesus is actually in the boat sleeping. A storm hit, and the disciples ran down the stairs and woke up the master. Jesus came up and calmed the wind and sea. But this time, Jesus decided that, rather than calm the sea from within the boat, I'm going to walk on it.

But because the disciples had allowed fear to rob them of their vision, they could not discern that God had put under his feet the very thing that was trying to defeat them!

Have you ever been in a situation where everything was going out of whack and everything seemed to be happening at once and you asked, "Where's God?" The problem was not that God wasn't there. He'd always been there. He never left. The problem is that we allowed the fear to make us call God, Satan.

Because of fear, there are times when God is working things out but we to start rebuking demons and devils. We believe the false notion that addition means God and subtraction means the devil. The truth is, there will be times we will experience subtraction and it will be from God. Just like there will be times that you will see addition but it's the devil trying to get you to fall into a trap. We believe if we don't get the exact answer to our petitions, God can't be speaking.

So during certain situations in our lives we find ourselves in darkness, in the middle of the sea, with winds blowing fiercely against us. And because we have lost our vision, our bearings, we rebuke Satan, not realizing that we're actually rebuking God for the work He is doing.

The reality is that we get ourselves in situations where there is no easy way out. We expect God to immediately dig us out of the hole we buried ourselves in. And when the hole gets deeper we panic. But that's because we don't see the whole problem the way God does.

◆——◆

God has us go deeper,
(he allows us to grow in faith)
he lets the problem get a little worse,
and then he shifts us

◆——◆

Some of us are dug in holes and we expect to go upwards but God sees when there is hard ground or large rocks above us, and if we just started going up, we'll be stuck. So instead God has us go deeper, (he allows us to grow in faith) he lets the problem get a little worse, and then he shifts us. Once we've pivoted and changed direction, he begins to pull us up against soft earth and not rocks.

Every Sunday alters get flooded with people asking for the preacher to lay hands on them so that God can take them out of what they are going through. But I am no longer going to be an accomplice to people fighting against God. It's time we figure out why are we in the messes we make in the first place. What do we need to learn?

The reason why God would allow us to be in situations like a storm, or in the middle of the sea, in the darkness with winds blowing fiercely against us, is because it's in those situations that He gets to show up and show off who He is. How can you know Jehovah Jireh (The Lord Will Provide), if your refrigerator was never empty or your bank account has never been in a negative? How would you ever know God as El Shaddai (God Almighty) if you never experience moments of weakness? How would you know Jehovah Rapha (The Lord who heals) if you never experience sickness in your body?

After Jesus speaks to the disciples and tells them to be of good cheer and to not be afraid because it is him, Peter answers Jesus and says, "Lord if it is you allow me that I come to you on the water."

Notice that out of all the disciples it's the fisherman that asked Jesus to walk on the water like him. It would've made more sense for another disciple, like Matthew or Phillip, to ask Jesus to walk on water, because they were not fishermen. Because Peter was a fisherman, he knew the dangers of the waters of the sea. Peter knew exactly what he was getting into.

That's why there is so much power in preaching the true gospel of the kingdom. The true gospel of the kingdom doesn't sell fairytales. It doesn't tell you if you come to Christ you're going to get a new car, a new house, and a big bank account. Can, and do Christians get these things? Of course. If you submit your finances to God, if you get educated on how to run your businesses, if you learn how to manage your money correctly, and, most importantly, if you love God more than money.

But when it comes to preaching the true gospel of the kingdom of God, Jesus said, "Pick up your cross and follow me." When a person knows exactly what they're getting into, and still makes the decision that this is the best thing that has ever happened to them, that's when you have a soul that has completely surrendered to God, and Jesus is living within them.

If there was anyone who had the skills to navigate that ship out of that storm, it was Peter. As a fisherman, Peter knew how to read the stars, how to read the size and shape of the moon, how to best handle the size of the waves, and how to best use the sails to manipulate the winds. But rather than him trying to take matters into his own hands, he decides to start walking towards Jesus, who didn't have the protection of the boat in the middle of a storm.

Many of us, because of the cards that life has dealt us, have learned how to survive. We've learned how to hustle for the family and loved ones. We're adept at fighting hard enough to make it another day. Because of this, we have the ability to see ourselves out of storms and contrary winds. But God is looking for people who will take the ability that they have to get out of their situation, and put it to the side and surrender completely to Jesus and go in.

Going in may mean going even deeper into the storm, or getting closer to the contrary winds. But it also means getting closer to Jesus. It means getting closer to Jesus through faith, believing in who He is, and that he rewards those who diligently seek him. Jesus is not on the outside looking in. When we allow it, He is right there with us. He's not looking at the waves that are thrashing you about, he's standing on top of them.

Peter asked Jesus that if it was he, to have him walk on water as Jesus was. But Peter did not attempt to walk on the water until Jesus told him, (verse 29) "come." Notice how in the passage the confusing matter, of whether it is a spirit or Jesus, had not been resolved. Peter himself is asking if you are our Lord, then have me walk on water as you are. But when Jesus told him to come, that was when Peter walked out of the boat. We must get to a place with God where is not about seeing God but hearing him.

I might not have good eyesight but if I have good hearing, and if I know you, I can still identify you. Most of us can tell who they're talking to by the person's voice. You could not be facing a door, and someone could walk in and say hello, and you'll know exactly who it is before seeing the person.

Too many of us are spiritually near-sighted and can't see when God is moving. On top of that they can't identify the voice of God.

If you recognize someone's voice on your phone, you first question won't be for him or her to prove it's really him or her, instead the question might be, "where are you calling from?" There would be no reason for proof of identity. When you know God's voice, you'll no longer waste time trying to identify if it's Him working or not. You will be using your time in prayer, seeking his face, in order to know what He wants you to do.

Peter knew that if the figure that was speaking was Jesus, all it needed was to speak a word and the impossible could happen. When the figure said come, Peter understood that it was his master. Because he knew Jesus' words. It was by a word that Jesus calmed the sea. It was by a word that He lifted up Gyrus' daughter from her deathbed. Peter just needed one word from his master, and he was ready to jump off the boat into a raging sea.

One of our biggest issues with God is that many times He would say to come or go, but will not give an explanation as to why. We would prefer God to sit down with us and tell us why he is telling us to do what he is telling us to do. The real problem begins when you refuse to move because God hasn't gotten into the specifics with you. You need to know that many times, God will only say come or go. The King of Kings and Lords of Lords is not into explaining to us, his creation,

His plans. He's not a God of explanations, He's a God of instructions. In due time the revelation of why he told you to do something a certain way, will be revealed to you.

God does not waste time. He likes getting things done

He does this because oftentimes He will ask you to do things that don't make sense to you. Your natural mind will have an impossible time trying to reason out His logic. That's because His thoughts are higher than ours. Why would He waste time trying to explain the way He does things to someone who can never understand His thought process? God does not waste time. He likes getting things done. He created everything on earth and above the earth in only six days. Our God does not waste time. But the awesome thing about God is that when we stop asking, and we start believing in who He is, it is then that He starts revealing. His goal is not for us to never understand why He wants us to do things certain ways or why He wants us to do something far out of our comfort zones. If you're in tune with him, he will reveal to you the entire panoramic picture of why He did everything the way He did.

When Peter walked out of the boat, and began to walk on water, notice that nowhere in the Bible does it say that the opposing winds stopped. This means that as Peter was attempting to get out the boat, the contrary winds are still present, trying to keep him in the boat. As Peter began to walk on water the contrary winds were trying to knock him off balance and send him into the tumultuous waves. The conditions had not changed.

I want you to understand what I'm about to say next because it's imperative for every believer to know this: Peter stepped onto a raging sea and against a howling wind. Every time the wind and seas got together the waves got higher. But the higher the waves got, the higher Peter got because he was on top of the waves! If the waves got higher than the boat, Peter got higher than the boat.

The people in the boat could only see the waves from their perspective, from inside the boat. But as the storm tried to intimidate Peter, by bringing him high up on the waves, Peter had a better vantage point than the people who thought had protection from the boat. As long as we can identify the Lord's voice, whatever is thrown at us will only work to elevate us. The higher the waves of attack from the enemy are, the higher the glory we will see.

Let's continue with the story. The Bible tells us in Matthew 14:30 that when Peter saw the boisterous winds he was afraid. It doesn't say when he saw the waves or when he heard the winds. It states, when he SAW THE WIND. How can you see the winds? The answer is, you can't in the natural but when you're in the supernatural, it's amazing the things you can see.

Even as Peter was experiencing something no mortal man ever experienced, walking on water, fear entered the equation. The spirit of fear has the ability to speak to you and make you visualize what it wants you to see. It tries to get you to see that you're not worth much. It tries to get you to see that you're not truly saved, that you'll never be a good Christian, that you'll always drink alcohol. The spirit of fear will try to get you to see that your marriage will always be rocky, that you'll never get ahead in life, and that you'll never be who God says you can be. Fear will point you to see the bad in a situation and not the good. Instead of Peter realizing what he was actually doing, that although the winds were hitting him hard and the waves were chaotic, he was still standing. Instead, he focused on the potency of the wind! The spirit of fear tries to get you stop walking and operating in the supernatural. The spirit of fear tries to bring you back down to the natural, for you to focus on what you can't do, and not focus on what God can do.

A while ago, I was counseling one of my church members, and he was telling me the difficulties he was going through. Totally distraught, he said to me, "I can't handle it anymore." He felt as if he was drowning in his marriage and finances and failing at keeping his emotions in check. He also felt he was failing in ministry. I let him speak, he needed to get everything off his chest. It hurt me to see someone I love feeling such sorrow and desperation.

I didn't join him in despair or offer up condolences for how he was feeling. Instead I spoke life to his situation. I reminded him of a conversation he and I had about four months prior. His eyes lit up as he recanted how God had been blessing him spiritually during that time. He talked of the peace that was in his home and how God had directed him on how to manage his finances.

When he finished I said, "You just told me that you feel you can't go on because of this and that and this. Let me ask you, weren't those same things going on four months ago when you were on fire for God?"

As his voice cracked with emotion he said, "Pastor, things were actually worse back them. I was open to everything I felt God was telling me to do. I was going from glory to glory and although the situations were worse, because I was really seeking the face of God, the same problems didn't seem so heavy."

Peter began to sink because he allowed fear to take away his vision, impair his hearing, and eat up his faith. When that happened all he had left was his own understanding. And his reasoning told him he had no business walking on water. The spirit of fear comes to rob you of your vision, to impair your hearing, and to eat up your faith so that you can base what is happening around you on your limited understanding.

According to your understanding, you are right, you have no business thinking that you're going to have a healthy marriage. You have no business believing that you're going to have peace. You have no business believing that you have a future that is completely disconnected from your past.

The spirit of fear will make you believe you are trying to operate in something you are not good at or worthy of. You are unqualified to be here. But to God, you are more than a conqueror. Through God the weak says, "I am strong." The enemy tries to overwhelm us with many words and with a lot of false information. The way God works is that He will usually give us a word at the beginning of the journey, and then the Holy Spirit that is within us will help us hold onto that Word as we are walking through the valley and through the desert, on our way to the promised land. It is during that time of the valley and the desert that the enemy usually shows up with many words to try to overwhelm us with information that is contrary to the Word that we received at the beginning of the journey.

Chapter 10

Sight vs. Vision

Peter allowed fear to rob him of his vision. When he lost his vision he shifted to sight. Vision had him locked on Jesus. Sight made him shift to seeing the boisterous winds. Verse 30 then says that when he was afraid, he began to sink, and cried, "Lord, save me." Notice how the Bible says that he *began* to sink.

When I was a child attending Sunday school, the teachers would give me a sheet to color on. On one of those sheets, I remember seeing the picture of Jesus walking on water, stretching out his hand towards Peter, as Peter was sinking into the water. In the picture, you could only see Peter's neck, head and a hand, while the rest of his body was already in the water. But the Bible says that Peter was beginning to sink, when immediately Jesus stretched forth his hand and caught him.

If you stepped off a boat and into deep water, you're head would be under the waves in less than fraction of a second. But many things happened when Peter was *beginning to sink.* He had time to cry out to the Lord to be saved. And Jesus had time to reach out and catch him. This is one of the least talked about miracles in the bible.

We need to understand that God is not confined to our concept of time. God slowed down time for Peter when he *began to sink.* People don't begin to sink, they just sink. But God had a plan for Peter. God wanted to use what was happening to teach the billions of believers in the centuries to come. So he didn't let Peter sink. Many times, we feel that we need an answer from God ASAP! That if He doesn't hurry up and make a way for us, we're going to drown. But time works for God, not the other way around. However, we get scared because the spirit of fear has us seeing the worst possible outcomes. Jesus had enough time to reach down and get a good hold of Peter's robes.

Time works for God, not the other way around

Notice how it says that Jesus caught Peter. It doesn't say that he lifted him up out of the water. The spirit of fear will make you think that things are worse than what they are. The spirit of fear wants to get you to drown in a cup of water. It wants to make you think that you've already drowned, when the water isn't even up to your knees. The reason the spirit of fear does this is because the enemy wants you to give up before the battle even ends.

The Bible says that as a man thinketh in his heart, so he is. The enemy knows that if he can defeat you in your mind, and in your spirit, and in your soul, he has already won. Peter didn't begin to sink and then became afraid. He first became afraid, and because he let fear in, he then began to sink. Many times we don't realize that it is not the situations in contrary winds we are facing that makes us afraid, it is that we've allowed the spirit of fear to enter and it is holding the door open for the winds to have an effect on our lives.

Verse 31 says that Jesus immediately stretched forth his hand, and caught him and said unto him, "ye of little faith, why did you doubt?" As we have mentioned before, the word fear comes from the same root word that means faithlessness. As Jesus is saving Peter he is also letting him know why he allowed the sinking to happen, and teaching him a lesson on how to defeat the spirit of fear. He is teaching Peter the very same lesson that Paul teaches Timothy years later in second of Timothy 1:4-7.

Faith destroys the spirit of fear. The perfect love of God casts out all fear. You see the love of God when Jesus immediately saves Peter, as he is beginning to drown. We see the lesson of faith when Jesus is telling Peter, as he is saving him from drowning, "man of little faith. Why did you doubt?" But as Jesus is teaching this lesson to Peter, notice that Jesus does this in a confidential, private, and intimate setting. The Bible says that the winds were boisterous. That means that the contrary winds were creating a lot of noise. It was also creating high waves.

As Peter is having this encounter with Jesus, the rest of the disciples are still in the same condition that they were at the beginning of the passage. They are still in the dark, in the middle of the sea, dealing with contrary winds creating high waves. Jesus teaches and rebukes Peter in private. Although Peter is struggling with the spirit of fear, Jesus does not expose his condition nor does he make public what he is going through. Jesus does this because even before Peter doubted Jesus and began to drown, He had already knew in his sovereignty that Peter would allow doubt and fear to enter.

This is why the Lord deals with you in private, intimate settings. I know that you been asking God, "Why do I feel so useless? Why am I not helping? Why am I not more in the public eye?" It's because God is dealing with your fear, with your doubt, and with your mess in a confidential setting. So that when God does place you in front of the multitude, they will not judge you according to your decisions and actions of the past.

Even though Jesus knew Peter would succumb to those spirits, He had already made up his mind on what type of guy Peter was. Jesus would later declare to Peter the he will be the rock on which the church was going to be founded on. Jesus had made this decision way before Peter starts to sink.

I tell you this to get you to understand that what Jesus has declared that you are, he has already taken into consideration not only what you have done but also what you will do. And none of these things changed God's mind about who He says you are. Romans 8:35, 37-39 declares, "who shall separate us from the love of Christ? Shall tribulation, or distress, or persecution, or famine, or nakedness, or peril, or sword (37)? Yet, in all things we are more than conquerors through him that loved us. For I am persuaded, that neither death, nor life, nor angels, nor principalities, nor powers, nor things present, nor things to come, nor height, nor depth, nor any other creature, shall be able to separate us from the love of God, which is in Christ Jesus our Lord."

There is nothing that you have done or can do that will change God's mind about who he says that you are!

The Bible tells us Peter had gotten off the boat to start walking towards Jesus. On his way there he begins to sink. But the Bible declares that as soon as he begins to sink and cries out help me Lord, Jesus immediately catches him. This means that Peter actually got pretty close to reaching Jesus. Because the Bible never says that Jesus goes towards Peter it simply says that he reached out his hand. That means that Peter was close enough for Jesus to simply reach out his had and catch Peter.

He's Always Closer Than You Think

The entire conversation — Peter asking if it's Jesus to Peter walking on the water - takes place in seconds. Jesus was far from them when the conversation started, that's why they couldn't identify him clearly. Yet, just a few moments later, Peter was walking on water. Then he began to sink. I don't think any of the disciples saw how fast Jesus was moving when Peter was walking on the water. They must have been focusing on Peter walking on the water. However, Jesus knew Peter was about to sink. When Peter started to sink, he cried out, he didn't reach for Jesus because he still thought Jesus was far away! But you need to understand that once you start walking in your promise, once you start walking in your calling, that although you might think Jesus is far from you, even though you've stumbled, even though you've fallen, he's just an arm's length away from you.

The spirit of fear wants us to focus more on how far we are from the shore rather than focus on how close we are to our destination. Although Peter did begin to sink, he also made it close enough to the master that Jesus could just reach out his hand and pick him up. He understood that the key wasn't for Jesus to come to him but for him to move towards Jesus. All Peter had to do was attempt to get close to the master and the master took care of the rest.

Peter then figures out the secret to overcoming the spirit of fear. Verse 32 says, "and when they were come into the ship, the wind ceased." The verse says "and when they, referring to Jesus and Peter. The Bible doesn't say Jesus carried Peter, he only helped him up. Peter didn't walk on water once. Peter walked on water twice. But the second time, he knew the secret to defeating the spirit of fear. The first time he walked towards Jesus. But the second time he walked *with* Jesus.

We have all these weapons of our warfare that are available to us. But none of them will work unless we are walking with Jesus. Walking with Jesus means that we operate according to His will and direction. We do it because Jesus said to. We say what we say because Jesus said to say it.

We get to the same place that Jesus himself got to with his father on the Mount of Olives. "Not my will be done. But Your will be done." That's the secret that unlocks all the power that is available to us as sons and daughters of God.

As we near the end of the story, let me tell you what happened to the wind. Once Peter and Jesus got on the boat, the wind ceased.

The wind no longer became a part of Peter's fear, it became a part of his testimony. Don't let the spirit of fear torment you, it's got nothing on you.

Tell fear, "Whatever you throw at me, I'm going to use for my testimony. And whoever will hear me will know that even when I thought I was sinking, even when you made my vision blurry, even when you came at me as an Antigen, I found my *dunamis* (power) in the name of Jesus and we have beaten you time and time again."

And before I conclude this book, let me prophesy to you. No longer will you be afraid of the spirit of fear. From here on out, fear will be afraid of you!

Acknowledgments

I would like to thank:

My editor and publisher, **Eli Gonzalez,** founder of The Ghost Publishing. Without you, this work would have never come about. Thank you for helping me convert this revelation into the powerful written word it is. You sir, don't have a gift from God, you are a gift from God.

Dr. Steve Robinson. Thank you for seeing potential in a boy from Harlem to change the world for Jesus. In an age when men are searching for spiritual fathers and mentors, you have been there for me as just that.

Bishop Herson Gonzalez for having the foresight of looking into the future and being an instrument used to push me into my purpose and destiny.

Pastor Rod Carpenter, from Redemption World Outreach Center for teaching me what the Kingdom of God is really about. Thank you for being a spiritual father from afar.

My mother for raising me and doing everything in her power to keep me from harm while living in a hostile environment. Our home was a "Mr. Roger's Neighborhood" in the middle of the hood. I love you Mom!

My brother in law, **Pastor Carlos Crespo** and sister in law, **Damaris Chesson**. Words could never express my love and gratitude for both of you. You are truly a brother and sister to me. Thank you for accepting me as family. Carlos, thank you for allowing me to be your spiritual father. Freedom church would not be what it is without either of you.

Lastly, but certainly not least, I'd like to thank my father, **Rinaldo "Paquito" Martinez.** As of the publishing date of this book, he will have celebrated 16 years of victory in heaven. I miss you dad. But I hope your little boy has made you proud. Thank you for being the best father a boy could hope for. It is an honor to look in the mirror, every day, and see you.

Recommended Reading

This is a list of just some of the books that have impacted my life greatly. I wholeheartedly recommend you read these books. They're great for the soul.

Necessity of an Enemy — *by Pastor Rod Carpenter*

On the Brink — *by Pastor Rod Parsley*

The Millennial Manual — *by Pastor Jay Patrick*

Walking in the Supernatural — *by Guillermo Maldonado*

About the Author

Pastor Lee Martinez is the Founder & President of The Chains Will Fall (TCWF) Ministries. He is also the Co-Founder and Co-Senior Pastor of Freedom Christian Church.

He currently resides in Leominster, MA with his wife Michelle and their six children — Richie, Danny, LJ, Leah, Micah, and Seth.

Pastor Lee and Michelle are dedicated to bringing about the Kingdom of God on earth. Their mission is to plant and grow churches under TCWF Ministries.

He considers himself a "huge" Stephan Curry and Golden State Warriors Fan and is a life-long New York Mets fan.

Pastor Lee's passion is to preach the word of God. He is a sought after preacher and speaker.

To contact him to speak or preach at your church, men's event, marriage conference, or youth event, contact him at: tcwfpastorlee@gmail.com.

Notes

Notes

Notes

_____

_____

_____

_____

_____

_____

_____

_____

_____

_____

Notes

_____

_____

_____

_____

_____

_____

_____

_____

_____

_____

_____

Notes

Notes

_____

_____

_____

_____

_____

_____

_____

_____

_____

_____

_____

Notes